CANNABIS CULTIVATION JOURNAL

A Complete Step-by-Step Guide
for Order, Efficiency, and Success

Allan J. Grajek

CANNABIS CULTIVATION JOURNAL
Copyright © 2018 by Allan J. Grajek

CONSCIOUS CREATIONS
PO Box 1627
Mendocino, CA 95460
Cannabiscultivationjournals.com
Cover and book design by Cypress House
Cover illustration copyright © Oleksii Koval/Alamy

The information in this book is intended strictly for educational purposes. If you apply the ideas herein, you are solely responsible for your choices, actions, and results. The author has made every effort to ensure that all the information was correct at time of publication; this is not, however, an exhaustive treatment of the subject matter. The author does not assume and hereby disclaims any liability to any party for any loss, damage, or disruption caused by errors or omissions, whether such errors or omissions result from accident, negligence, or any other cause. The content provided does not take the place of expert legal advice from your attorney.

ISBN 978-1-7322372-0-9
LCCN: 2018951439

PRINTED IN THE USA
2 4 6 8 9 7 5 3 1
First edition

DEDICATION

To all who have worked and sacrificed to bring the world
an awareness of this plant's great potential and healing power.

CONTENTS

PART 1 — CULTIVATION   1

PREFACE

THIS JOURNAL is presented in three parts:

1. Cultivation;
2. Harvesting; and
3. Post-Harvest.

You can use sticky tabs and paper clips to mark the different sections of the journal, and can also use them to mark particular pages that you reference frequently.

To make optimal use of this journal you'll need to label each plant by number once you've sexed, selected, and planted them for production (see page 35). This will enable you to record and reference specific details about the progress of each plant. Before they're sexed and selected, you can label them by their strain. Further guidelines for labeling are given throughout the journal. There are also a few pages designated for charting the layout of the garden such that each numbered plant may be arranged on a map for easy reference and location. The materials for journaling include a pen with waterproof ink, a pencil, a ruler, sticky tabs, and some colored paper clips.

In just minutes each day, you can organize and track the progress of your entire operation. Keeping a journal evokes mindfulness and is like having an external memory storage aiding in the prevention and solution of mysteries from the garden to the drying room. A record of daily activities and discoveries can serve as a guide for creating a daily or weekly agenda. It can help you keep track of the plants and their individual needs, and can provide a reference for future cultivation. This guide includes tips for labeling, a conversion chart, a place for garden maps, watering and feeding charts, and a section to record and track the finished product. Feel free to tailor any of the methods or instructions within to suit your needs. I hope this journal will bring ease, harmony, and prosperity to your agricultural endeavor.

I have a PDF containing all the worksheets in the book, available free for people who've purchased the book. Go to **cannabiscultivationjournals.com** and click on "Contact." Email me your request for the forms and include a note regarding where you purchased the book.

ACKNOWLEDGMENTS

FIRST AND FOREMOST, my love and gratitude to the One who created me and provides for me.

I am grateful to all those who've helped me along this path: To my father for my work ethic; special thanks to my brother Eric for believing in me; to my brother Christopher for inspiring me to reach high; super-big thanks to Mom for all the support, friendship, and wise guidance you've generously shared throughout my life; to my dear friend Margie, for your patience, support, and encouragement; to every teacher I've been graced to learn from; and last but not least, my humble gratitude to the angels and spirits of the cannabis plants for the healing, guidance, and friendship you consistently share.

PART 1—
CULTIVATION

PROPER PLANNING

YOU CAN USE the next two pages to jot down plans of action and supplies needed, including soil, estimated costs, and responsibilities. Imagine you're getting ready to begin a project. What do you need and when do you need it? If you're sharing responsibilities, write down who is responsible for what and when. You can make notes about the sequence of necessary actions and the order in which various supplies will be needed. Create methods that will help you identify key features, such as circling costs or numbering and underlining the sequence in which actions must be taken. After these two pages, two more are provided to organize your notes, so don't worry if it seems to get disorderly.

PROPER PLANNING

PROPER PLANNING

THE NEXT TWO pages are reserved for the organization of your lists of needs and your plans of action. You might want to divide your supplies, costs, and responsibilities into the phases in which they will be used and or needed, e.g., seed starting, vegging, flowering, and harvesting.

PROPER PLANNING

PROPER PLANNING

SEED STARTING

HERE YOU CAN list the variety of strains that you're going to start, where they came from, or who produced them, anything about their origin, how old they are, and any other information you find important.

Assign each strain a symbol or an abbreviation that works for you. These symbols or abbreviations can be used when labeling seed starts and for recording information later on in this journal. Parenthesize each initial and make a note as to what each stands for. There is a page provided on p. 21 to serve as a key to transfer the symbols, abbreviations, and initials along with their prospective meanings for easy referencing.

Example:

Kashmir Kush (KK) from my buddy Mr. S;

Cherry pie = (CP) from Boonville, 2 yrs old;

Kashmir Kush = (KK1) from guys in Oregon

SEED STARTING

_____
_____
_____
_____
_____
_____
_____
_____
_____
_____
_____
_____
_____
_____
_____
_____
_____
_____
_____
_____
_____
_____
_____
_____
_____
_____
_____
_____
_____
_____

SEED STARTING

SEED SOWING AND GERMINATION

RECORD WHICH STRAINS, how many seeds of each, and the date you started them. Include information about the method of germination, the temperature, the moon cycle, how long it took each strain to germinate, the ratio of survival, and your personal well-being. If planting directly into soil, include information about what kind of soil you used and in what size pots.

Leave some space to record the male/female ratio once you've sexed all the plants. More often than not the male/female ratio has to do with the parents, but sometimes it has to do with the conditions under which the seedlings have been grown. Recording the details of these conditions and comparing any differences year to year might give you some important clues as to why you are getting the results you're getting. This may help you to decide where to get seeds in the future, but most important, this information will help you to get to know each strain and see which ones work best for you and how you can work best for them.

Example:

(2/15/18) started 50 seeds of KK1 on the new moon at midnight in damp paper towels. Ambient temp. = 76 degrees Fahrenheit. Seeds split in 24 hours. In three days the tails were 2 inches long; 88% survival rate. Played "The Beatles" all day long. 65% male 35% female.

SEED SOWING AND GERMINATION

Sprout Planting

RECORD THE DATE, time of day, moon cycle, temperature, air pressure, type of soil, amendments, and any details of your method that you think might be of importance. How many sprouts were planted, and how long did the task take, including the soil preparation? How many people assisted? Including information that explains the details of the plants' environment may be helpful when assessing their progress. Are they in the shade or full sun, natural light or artificial?

This list might also include all the supplies, nutrients, and implements involved, including which tools were helpful or a hindrance, information about how you were doing, the energy of the day, and other pertinent information.

Label the sprouts with tags using abbreviations and symbols, and then record that info here. Use symbols to mark individual plants that show anomalies or may have been damaged while transplanting. This will help you to keep track of individuals and see how well they recover. Transfer data in reference to the symbols to the "key" on p. 21

Continue recording data here until the seedlings have been transplanted.

Example:

2/20/18 – 75 (KK) sprouts planted into six-packs in the AM. Temp between 65 and 76. Seed starter mix with 25% worm castings. In full sun. Planted on a root day of the moon cycle. Took 3 hours to accomplish by myself. Feeding water and light fish-emulsion solution. Tweezers and pencil worked great for planting. Played Indian sitar music and was in a great mood. Three sprouts got damaged during planting; each is marked with an "X."

SPROUT PLANTING

Sprout Planting

Transplanting

This section is for you to record the details of all the transplantation that may take place from germination to the final planting. Separate and label each transplanting period by sequence, i.e., 1st transplanting, 2nd transplanting, and so on. Here you can keep track of when transplants took place, watering and feeding schedules, range of ambient temperatures, what procedure and materials were used, what kind of soil and what size pots, and how much the plants appear to grow every few days. Are you keeping them on heating mats? What's their light source? Which ones are growing faster than others? Add any details that you think may be important.

Use symbols to differentiate various qualities and anomalies. Whatever symbol you choose to use doesn't really make a difference. The idea is to provide a means of easily labeling and tracking the progress of individual plants. Use an exclamation mark (!) to designate injured plants, a dollar symbol ($) for plants that seem extra-vigorous, or a caret (^) for plants that seem to be growing slowly. Label individual plants that catch your attention for one reason or another. Some may be attractive to you while others might express an anomaly that you feel you should keep an eye on. For instance, one of the seedlings seems to be growing in an odd way compared to the rest. A label with the initials of the seedlings' genetics and a symbol representing its oddity would be assigned to that plant. If you discover other seedlings with similar oddities, you would label them with the same symbol along with the initials of their genetics. However you choose to label and mark these plants, write it down here so you can follow up on them in the coming phases of this journal. This information may help you discern which plants you'd like to select for your crop, and can also give you insight as to which details to pay attention to for next year's selection.

Example:

Tues., March 20, transplanted 100 (KK) and 77 (AFG) seedlings into 4-inch pots of a growers blend containing 3 parts soil to 1 part live worm castings. Transplanted them in the morning, and the moon was in a good phase for root growth. Five of the KK starts had weird, wrinkled leaves and I marked them with an *; 10 of the KKs were just glowing, so I marked them with the $. // On March 29 I noticed that 7 of the AFG seedlings had already begun to grow branches. They look really healthy, and I'm marking these as my favorites with a five-pointed star. // March 30: I came in this morning and all looked a bit pale, so I gave them some fish emulsion mixed with water. // April 1: everybody's looking much greener today. My favorites are still in the lead, and the odd ones are looking more odd. // April 3: three of the AFG seedlings appear to have white stripes on the leaves; I marked them with an "X" to remind me to pay close attention.

Transplanting

TRANSPLANTING

TRANSPLANTING

Key to Symbols, Initials, and Abbreviations

This page is reserved for the translation of all of the symbols, initials, and abbreviations used throughout the book. It may be used as key to reference whenever there's question as to what any of these characters mean. This is especially helpful when translating the map, which will mainly be marked with numbers and symbols.

Example:

KK = Kashmir Kush from Mr. S * = wrinkled seed leaves

KK1 = Kashmir Kush from Oregon $ = fast growing

CP = Cherry pie   ★ = my favorites

AFG = Afghan Goo   X = pay close attention

You'll reference this section often, so keep it organized, orderly, and easy to read.

SEXING

WHEN SEXING, this section allows you to take note of how many plants you designated male or female in correlation with their genetics.

Example:

STRAIN	DATE	MALES	FEMALES	STRAIN	DATE	MALES	FEMALES
KK1 =	(5/14/18)	15 males	6 females				
CP =	(5/14/18)	10 males	4 females				

SEXING

STRAIN	DATE	MALES	FEMALES	STRAIN	DATE	MALES	FEMALES

SEXING

STRAIN	DATE	MALES	FEMALES	STRAIN	DATE	MALES	FEMALES

GENERAL NOTES REGARDING INDIVIDUAL STRAINS

NOTE ANY DETAILS about the individual strains that you found interesting or of importance while tending to the plants along their way up to the present moment. What is the level of health and vigor of each strain? Did one strain need more or less of something? Did any seem more or less resistant to stress? What phenotypes are prominent? You can also include the male-to-female ratio and the source they came from.

GENERAL NOTES REGARDING INDIVIDUAL STRAINS

MALES

USE THIS PAGE to record specific details about any males you might choose to cultivate. Include information about their genetics, when they flowered, and the specific phenotypes of each.

WATERING, FEEDING, AND MAINTENANCE

THE NEXT FEW pages are designed for you to chart your watering and feeding history.

Below is a conversion chart for your convenience. These measurements are close approximations, and may vary slightly from substance to substance.

- 1 tsp = .16 fl. oz = 4.7 g. = 4.92 ml

- 3 tsp = 1 tbsp = .5 fl. oz. = 14.3 g. or 14.7 ml

- 2 tbsp = ⅛ cup = 1 fl. oz. = 28.3 g. or 29.5 ml

- 4 tbsp = ¼ cup = 2 fl. oz. = 56.7 g. or 59.14 ml

- 8 tbsp = ½ cup = 4 fl. oz. = 113.4 g. or 120 ml

- 16 tbsp = 1 cup = 8 fl. oz. = 127 g. = 240 ml

- 64 tbsp = 4 cups = 1qt = 32 fl. oz = 907.2 g. = 960 ml

- 256 tbsp =4 qt = 1 gallon = 128 fl. oz = 3660.8 g. = 3785.4 ml

Use the following page to record the amounts of ingredients to gallons of water you used during any given phase, whether for feeding nutrients or foliar spraying. For instance, if you use a 100-gallon reservoir for your nutrient solution, you'd write how many cups of fish emulsion to add to each reservoir, and so on. Include the order in which nutrients should be mixed into the reservoir, the date, and which week of the plant's cycle each preparation is for; i.e., week 1 of the vegetative phase or week 3 of the flowering phase. As the measurements and ingredients change, simply cross out the earlier notes and make new ones.

Use the maintenance chart on page 30 to briefly describe how the plants were cared for on each day or use this chart to plan and arrange an agenda of tasks on the dates they need to be fulfilled. This can help eliminate the possibility of over- or under-watering and feeding. It can also help you plan ahead and delegate tasks on a day-to-day basis. To make optimal use of the space provided, use symbols in place of words. Remember to log the symbols in the key for reference.

WATERING, FEEDING, AND MAINTENANCE

WATERING AND MAINTENANCE CHART

	APRIL	MAY	JUNE	JULY
01	Veg. Nutrients			
02	Foliar Fed			
03	Watered / Minerals			
04	No water			
05	Water + Nutrient			
06	Transplanted			
07				
08				
09				
10				
11				
12				
13				
14				
15				
16				
17				
18				
19				
20				
21				
22				
23				

Watering and Maintenance Chart

	April	May	June	July
24				
25				
26				
27				
28				
29				
30				
31				

	August	September	October	November
01				
02				
03				
04				
05				
06				
07				
08				
09				
10				
11				
12				
13				

WATERING AND MAINTENANCE CHART

	AUGUST	SEPTEMBER	OCTOBER	NOVEMBER
14				
15				
16				
17				
18				
19				
20				
21				
22				
23				
24				
25				
26				
27				
28				
29				
30				
31				

WATER USAGE

RECORD THE AMOUNT of water used during any given phase of the garden's life cycle. Note how many gallons of water are used per plant in accordance with how many gallons of soil each is being grown in. This information can be helpful when planning for or expanding next year's crop.

PHASE OF GROWTH	WATER PER PLANT	GALLONS OF SOIL
Week 12 of veg.	10 gallons	200

Water Usage

PHASE OF GROWTH	WATER PER PLANT	GALLONS OF SOIL

RESPECTIVE CHARACTERISTICS

THIS SECTION IS for recording a variety of details about each individual plant. It is optional, and its uses can be varied. Those growing hundreds of plants can use this section to record specific data about particular plants of special care. If you plan on propagating, you can also use it to make note of plants with favorable phenotypes.

To begin, you need to assign each plant a number. This is important because it allows you to keep track of individual plants and the product each produces. Also, the numbers serve as a reference for clear communication between master gardener and cultivation operatives.

ASSIGNING PLANT NUMBERS: Wait until all the selected plants are positioned and planted where they will be for the duration of the project. Once they're planted, find a good starting point and begin to count them in a way that's convenient and easy to follow. For example, if the plot is set up in rows, start at the beginning of a row at one end of the garden, and count all the plants in that row, then hop directly across to the next row and continue counting. Proceed in this manner until all the plants in that plot are accounted for. It should wind up looking like a zigzag if you were to connect the dots in sequence from #1 to the finishing number (see sample maps, pages 50 and 51) If you're growing in more than one plot or greenhouse, you can make a distinction between plots by assigning each a letter. When labeling plants from various plots, give each a number and the letter in association with the plot on which it's being grown. For example, plants in plot A would be labeled #1a, #2a, #3a, etc.; plants from plot B would be labeled #1b, #2b, #3b, etc.

This type of labeling can help you find your way around the garden and also enables operatives to follow up on particular maintenance plans for individual plants as well as for individual plots.

For the following pages, allot at least four lines to each plant, and indicate the start of each block with a bullet point. Write down the plant number, its initials, and any symbols that pertain to that plant. Transfer any potentially important previous records concerning each plant, and include any of the following information that might be helpful.

- The date when they first show signs of gender or first begin to flower.

- Specific needs pertaining to nutrients.

- When to stop feeding vegetative nutrients.

- Favorable phenotypes such as color, smell, or size.

- When they should be flushed.

- When to begin feeding phosphorus.

- Predictions on when you think they should finish.

- When they're harvested for the 1st, 2nd, and 3rd cuttings.

- If for any reason they appear unwell.

- If they seem sensitive to certain nutrients.

- How much soil they're being grown in.

- Anything else that you think could be important.

This information can be helpful when assessing daily strategies and planning harvest tasks before going out to the field.

Example:

(#25b KK) ☆ Gets full sun. 1st to flower and should be 1st to finish.

Has a small spot of crown rot. Switching to flower food on Aug. 21.

Seems to be very sensitive to strong nutrients, so feed lightly and water well between feedings.

Very strong, healthy genetics.

RESPECTIVE CHARACTERISTICS

RESPECTIVE CHARACTERISTICS

RESPECTIVE CHARACTERISTICS

RESPECTIVE CHARACTERISTICS

RESPECTIVE CHARACTERISTICS

RESPECTIVE CHARACTERISTICS

RESPECTIVE CHARACTERISTICS

RESPECTIVE CHARACTERISTICS

Respective Characteristics

Respective Characteristics

RESPECTIVE CHARACTERISTICS

GENERAL NOTES

THIS SPACE IS provided for recording any data you might find important for future reference. Which plants had strong branches? Which ones evidenced greater resistance to infestations such as mold or mites? Which strains needed more or less nutrients? Which were easier to maintain for one reason or another? Which produced more or less? These are just a few of the questions that might help you decide which strains will work best for you in the future.

GARDEN MAP

ONCE YOU'VE NUMBERED the plants, you can make a map of the garden space. The size and design of this map will depend on the size of your garden and can be laid out in many ways. However large or how many plots it consists of, I suggest you scale it down such that the entire layout can fit onto one page. Then make a separate map of each individual plot.

If a plot is too large to fit onto one page, separate the map into northern and southern or eastern and western regions. To indicate each plant on the map, use a circle about the size of a half-dollar coin, though it may be as small as a penny. Once you've drawn the circles in their relative places, write the corresponding numbers and initials in each. Use scratch paper to draft maps, and then copy them onto the blank pages that follow the sample maps on the next pages. Make a few extra copies of each of your maps, so you can post them in places of usefulness. These maps make it easy and convenient to plan and to delegate a variety of tasks.

SAMPLE MAP 1

NORTH

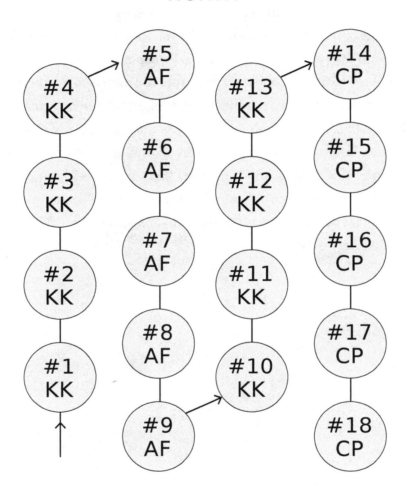

Note: This page is intended to serve as an example, and can be discarded after use.

SAMPLE MAP 2

SOUTH

Note: This page is intended to serve as an example, and can be discarded after use.

Garden Map

Garden Map

GARDEN MAP

Pests and Infestations

Take note of harmful pests and infestations such as spider mites, russet mites, broad mites, thrips, powdery mildew, black mold, crown rot, or aphids. Using the map and the numbers of individual plants, clarify where the pests were spotted and on which plants. Describe the process and the action taken to remedy the situation, including the dates and timeframes. Make a note of which plants to keep a close eye on. Write down which products and methods were effective and which were not, and make a note of when to apply any products as a follow-up action to prevent reinfestation. Record any information about the pests and their life cycles that you think could be useful.

The master gardener and maintenance operatives should review this section regularly to remain aware of the whereabouts of infestations and the practices needed to eradicate and prevent them from spreading.

Example:

Spider mites found in the NW corner of the garden on plants #7 and #15. Sprayed neem on them and the surrounding plants 7/10/18. Spray again on 7/14, then again on 7/18. Pay close attention to them and the surrounding plants for the next two weeks.

PESTS AND INFESTATIONS

PART 2 —
HARVESTING

HARVESTING ASSESSMENTS AND
DAILY HARVESTING AGENDA

THE FOLLOWING PROCEDURES are designed for gardens that consist mainly of seed starts or a variety of clones. If the garden consists mainly of the same kinds of clones, then you can use the space in this section in whichever way works best for you to create a daily program. However you choose, the guidelines provided here serve as examples to give you ideas as to how to stay on track and remain organized throughout the harvest.

As the harvest season begins, examine all your plants to get an idea of the sequence in which they'll be ready. Record the date of assessment, the plant number or strain, and any brief details of importance. Note which plants are to be harvested immediately, which are next in line for harvest, and what to keep a close eye on. If you harvest plants in parts, as opposed to harvesting entire plants at once, include details as to which harvest you're referring to, such as "1st," "2nd," or "3rd" harvest.

Mention key details about plants that must soon be examined; e.g., plants #1, 5, and 9 look very close to being ready; plants #18 and 20 probably have a few more days, but I'm concerned about mold; check on them again tomorrow. Plant #22 has about 15% amber trichomes and should be watched closely (see "Harvesting Assessments" example, page 61).

Once you've finished all the individual assessments, organize your data and create a daily harvesting agenda. Arrange items for the next 24 to 48 hours in the order in which they need to be carried out. (See "Harvesting Agenda" example page 66). Again ...Note which plants are to be harvested, which are next in line for harvest, and what to keep a close eye on. Taking note of what's to be harvested within the next few days can help you to plan ahead and coordinate the appropriate preparations. Include the date along with information explaining how much or which parts of each plant need to be harvested. Your notes might look a bit like this:

(Oct. 8) The tops of plants #33, 22, and 15 look ready and should be harvested tomorrow morning at the latest.

(Oct. 9) 1st harvest; tops only for plants #33, 22, and 15.

Or, your notes might look something like this:

(Oct. 9) <u>1st harvest plants #33, 22, 15, and 1.</u> // Plant #18 is not quite mature, but I found a bit of mold on it, so harvest just the main cola buds and mark them for closer inspection. // <u>2nd harvest plants #2, 7, and 11.</u> By the end of the day, check on plants #4, 5, and 8; they're almost ripe but might have a few days left.

If you harvest plants whole, your notes might look something like this:

(Oct. 10) <u>Harvest plants #10, 15, 22, and 34.</u> Mold was found intermittently on each plant, so these should be closely inspected as they are processed for drying. Plants #20, 21, 23, 25, and 27 need to be harvested tomorrow. // Keep a close eye on the OG strains, including plants #3, 4, 8, 12, and 24. They aren't looking completely mature but may be beginning to stretch. Plants #1, 2, 7, 9, 11, 14, and 18 have about three weeks to go and should be fed once more by tomorrow. We'll need a few more farmhands on duty for tomorrow's harvest.

(Also see example, page 61).

Notice how two forward slashes are used to separate different sets of notes that appear under the same date. Notice too how the plants to be harvested are underlined to signify that those plants are to be, or were, harvested on that date. Easy identification of this information, and clear distinction between the chores of the day, can be helpful when deciphering and referencing these notes. Also, knowing when plants were harvested can provide clues to solving mysteries. If, for instance, a product loses its label during the drying process, you can often look into this section and deduce what the product is by seeing which plants were harvested in the same timeframe and comparing that information with what product still has its label.

This method can save a lot of time, and gives you an idea of what to look for each day; also, if you share the responsibilities of this process, or have to be absent for a few days, it can allow someone else to see where you left off and easily step in to sub for you.

The details of these assessments may also be of help by providing the harvesting operatives the information they need to prepare the appropriate labels for the daily harvest ahead of time. Steps like this can help to keep order and expedite the process.

For instance one could refer to the Daily Harvesting Agenda and then make out the labels accordingly; each label would display the date of harvest, the plant number, strain initials, and which phase of harvest. If there's any concern about mold, mark the label with a question mark and the letter "M." This will indicate a need for further inspection while being processed.

Example:

```
?M
10/7
#3KK
2nds
```

NOTE: WHEN PREARRANGING your daily harvest activities, refer to the garden map section, pages 49-54 regarding how to locate specific plants. Once any plant is completely reaped, mark an "X" through that plant on the map.

Harvesting Assessments

Example:

10/06/18
(#1) Has a while; check again next week.
(#2) Ready / Harvest today / 1st harvest.
(#3) Harvest tomorrow / 2nds.
(#4) Keep an eye on / getting close.
(#5) Keep an eye on.
(#8) A week to go. Check for mold daily.
(#9) Looking very close; check again tomorrow.

10/10/18
(#17) Check again tomorrow
(#18) Keep an eye out for mold; the plant's a bit under-ripe, but the tops might have to be harvested early.
(#19) At least 2 weeks left.
(#20) A week to go. Check for mold tmrw.
(#22) 15% amber; check again in 3 days.

HARVESTING ASSESSMENTS

Harvesting Assessments

HARVESTING ASSESSMENTS

HARVESTING ASSESSMENTS

DAILY HARVESTING AGENDA
WHAT'S READY / NEXT IN LINE / KEEP A CLOSE EYE ON

Example:

(10/06/18) 1st harvest plant #2. // Harvest seconds for #3 tomorrow.

(10/07/18) 2nd harvest #3. // Examine plants #4 and 5 in the evening.

(10/09/18) 1st harvest #33, 32, and 15. // 2nd harvest #2, 7, and 11.

Daily Harvesting Agenda

DAILY HARVESTING AGENDA

Daily Harvesting Agenda

Daily Harvesting Agenda

PART 3 —
POST-HARVEST

DRYING AND CURING

YOU CAN USE this section as a scratch sheet for any kind of note you'd like to leave for yourself or other operatives during the drying and curing stage of production. Use this page to keep track of what's still in the drying room, what has moved on and to where. If, for example, a few boxes of product were to get moved from the drying room for further curing, you would make a note displaying the date, the number of boxes moved, where they were moved to, and what strains or plants they contained (see example a).

You can also use this section during the curing process to keep track of product that needs to be temporarily closed up, and product that needs to be opened to breathe and when to check on it again. For example, I like to separate the product into groups according to how dry or moist it is. As each group gets closer to being finished, I temporarily put them in an airtight container, usually a cardboard box lined with a food-grade plastic bag. Sometimes I have as many as fifteen boxes in a group containing as many as seven different strains. Here I would mark how many boxes were in the group, which strains were included, and how long to wait before returning to check on them. Each time you check on a group, make a note of it along with instructions as to when it should be checked again (see example b).

When you're done using notes, simply cross them out with a pencil. Keep in mind that you might need this information as a reference, so don't cross it out in a way that makes it illegible. Different sets of notes can be distinguished from one another by drawing a line between each. Note how punctuation marks are used to distinguish information, e.g., how a double forward slash is used to separate daily information.

SCRATCH SHEET AND TO-DO LIST

Example a:

10/19/17 – moved (12 boxes) from the drying room to curing room, containing plants #1, 5, 10, and 13.

Example c:

10/20/17 – Plant #3 is hanging in the drying room and should come down tomorrow. This is the 2nd cutting of this plant, so remember to combine it with the 1st cutting once it's dry enough.

Example b:

10/21/17 – (14 boxes) containing plants #1, 7, 8, 21, 18, 6 are closed and need to be checked in two days. // 10/23/17 – checked and left opened. Check again tomorrow. // 10/24 checked and left to be closed until they get manicured.

Example d:

10/22 – (×5 brown bags) of trimmed product containing #10 and 13 are in the curing room. Not yet recorded, still need about 2 days of drying time before bagging and tagging.

SCRATCH SHEET AND TO-DO LIST

SCRATCH SHEET AND TO-DO LIST

THE MANICURING PHASE

THIS IS A scratch sheet for recording what's being manicured at the moment. This helps managers and other operatives to easily reference where product is. For instance, if a person in charge of the drying room needs to combine recently dried parts of plant #33 with parts that were dried the week before, he or she can look at the records to find where they are. Or, if a product has been manicured and not yet been recorded as bagged and tagged, it could be easily located. The drying and curing process can be a complex and sometimes chaotic undertaking. Records that contain the location of the product throughout the process are key to limiting confusion and resolving mysteries.

When manicuring, write down the date and the strain type or the numbers of the product being worked on as they're distributed. Using parentheses to isolate the date helps distinguish it from the numbers of the plants being manicured. If the product was harvested in stages, be sure to make a note of which stage is being manicured; i.e., the 1st, 2nd, or 3rd harvest. This will signify if the product needs to be reserved so it can later be mixed with the rest of the produce associated with that plant or strain. Combining produce from the 1st, 2nd, and 3rd harvests will provide a well-rounded product containing both the large cola buds from the 1st harvest and smaller ones from the 3rd.

PRESENTLY BEING MANICURED

Example:

(10/29) – #1, #7, #13. All 1st harvest.

(10/30) – #13, 2nd harvest, #8 whole
plant including 1st, 2nd, and 3rd cuttings.

> **Note:** Typically, you wouldn't need to signify that
> "whole plant" means 1st, 2nd, and 3rd cuttings;
> I mention it here for the clarity of the example.

(11/1) – #8 2nd and 3rd harvest // #10
2nd harvest // #14 whole plant
(or simply WP).

PRESENTLY BEING MANICURED

PRESENTLY BEING MANICURED

PRESENTLY BEING MANICURED

BAGGED AND TAGGED

THIS SECTION IS for recording the weight of all product that has been processed and packaged. For example, once the product is done being prepared, it can be weighed out, packaged, and recorded. Leave a copy of this form F-1 with the person bagging and tagging to keep a record of things as they are bagged and tagged. Record the date, plant number, strain, and date. Transfer the information to this journal when convenient.

Example:

Date	Strain	Weight	Date	Strain	Weight
11/03	#28 (PK)	15 lb-347g			
11/04	#22 (PK)	3 lb			
11/04	#22 (Afg)	2.5 lb			

Total weight for this page:_____   Date_____

BAGGED AND TAGGED (FORM F-1)

Date	Strain	Weight	Date	Strain	Weight

TOTAL WEIGHT PRODUCED

Total product weight produced: _____   Date _____

In Stock

KEEP TRACK OF inventory by writing down what enters and leaves your storage facility. Two forms are provided for this: F-2 and F-3. Copies of form F-2 can be left in the storage facility, and F-3 stays with the journal. Transfer the inventory balances from forms F-2 to F-3 at the end of each day. Having these records in the journal will allow you to be aware of what's in stock without having to go to the storage facility.

DIRECTIONS FOR FORM F-2 (EXAMPLE A)

ALLOT ONE STRAIN per grid. As product comes into the storage facility, record the date and its weight in the "Incoming" field. Applying the date when items come in or leave can help solve questions if mistakes are made on any of the other forms.

As product leaves the storage facility, record its weight and the present date in the "Outgoing" field.

Next, write down the total weight of that particular strain in the "In Stock" field. Any equations necessary as inventory comes in or leaves the facility can go into this field as well; just make sure to underline or circle the available balance for easy referencing. As new balances are written in, simply cross out the previous ones.

As each grid gets full, simply transfer the strain name and the total weight remaining in stock to an empty grid on the same form and resume recording as indicated.

Note: It's necessary to transfer only the date and records of what's presently in stock (see example a2).

INCOMING	OUTGOING	IN STOCK
Purple Kush (11/03) 15 lb and 347 g.; (11/04) 3 lb; (11/5) 6 lb; (11/12) 3 lb	(11/09) 9lb (11/11) 13 lb	15 lb 347 g. + 3 = 18 lb/ 347 g.; + 6 = 24 lb/347 g.; −9 lb = 15 /347; −13 lb = 2 lb/347 g.; + 3 = 5/347
Afghan (11/04) 2.5 lb; (11/13) 2 lb;	(11/11) 1 lb	2.5 lb −1 lb = 1.5 lb; + 2 lb = 3.5 lb

Example a2: In this example, the strain name and remaining weight in stock was transferred from the "Purple Kush" field in example a.

INCOMING	OUTGOING	IN STOCK
Purple Kush		5 lb/347 g.

FORM F-2

INCOMING	OUTGOING	IN STOCK

FORM F-2

INCOMING	OUTGOING	IN STOCK

FORM F-2

INCOMING	OUTGOING	IN STOCK

-

-

-

-

-

-

DIRECTIONS FOR FORM F-3 (SEE EXAMPLE B)

- ➤ Transferring information from example a, form F-2, to form F-3.

- ➤ Transfer the name of the strain into the "Strain" field.

- ➤ Transfer how much of that strain remains in stock into the "In Stock" field.

- ➤ As new balances come in, simply cross out the previous ones. Any math involved can be done on form F-2.

This information will allow you to see what's in stock without having to go to the storage facility. If more space is needed to transfer information, you can make copies of form F-3 and insert them into this section.

When a grid is full or an item goes out of stock, lightly cross it out with a pencil.

Example b: Form F-3 Transference of information from form F-2, example a, onto form F-3. Information transferred on two separate occasions.

STRAIN	IN STOCK
• Purple Kush	~~(11/4) 18 lb/347 g.~~ (11/12) 5 lb/347 g.

FORM F-3

STRAIN	IN STOCK
•	
•	
•	
•	
•	
•	

FORM F-3

STRAIN	IN STOCK
•	
•	
•	
•	
•	
•	

FINISHED WEIGHT OF EACH PLANT

THIS SECTION IS primarily for projects consisting of large plants, or for keeping track of the production ability of different strains and / or the effectiveness of different types of nutrients. For example, plants of the same strain may be fed different nutrients as an experiment to see which nutrients works best; or plants of different strains could be fed the same nutrients to see which ones yield the most. It can also give one an idea as to how much weight to expect in the future from particular sizes of plants growing in particular amounts of soil. There are many ways you can use this chart, form F-4, to enhance your knowledge and cultivation experience. Record the plant number and / or strain, the weight it produced and how many gallons of soil it was grown in.

Example:

#1 Afghan/Goo
3.7 lb/ 100 gal.

FORM F-4

DATE OF THE GROWING CYCLE = DATE: _____ TO _____

F-4

FORM F-4

DATE OF THE GROWING CYCLE = DATE: _____ TO _____

F-4

GENERAL NOTES

TOTAL WEIGHT OF EACH STRAIN

USE THIS PAGE to record the total weight produced by each strain. Include any information you think might be useful for future referencing.

STRAIN SUMMARY

EXAMPLE:

STR: #9 Afghan/Goo	STR:
THC: 28% CBD: 1%	THC: CBD:
INDICA/SATIVA: 80/20	INDICA/SATIVA:
AROMA: Musky with a hint of cherry pie.	AROMA:
TASTE: Earthy and sweet with a hint of citrus	TASTE:
POTENCY: moderately strong	POTENCY:
EFFECT: energizing and relaxing.	EFFECT:
APPEARANCE: Big buds, dark green, brown hairs	APPEARANCE:
STR:	STR:
THC: CBD:	THC: CBD:
INDICA/SATIVA:	INDICA/SATIVA:
AROMA:	AROMA:
TASTE:	TASTE:
POTENCY:	POTENCY:
EFFECT:	EFFECT:
APPEARANCE:	APPEARANCE:
STR:	STR:
THC: CBD:	THC: CBD:
INDICA/SATIVA:	INDICA/SATIVA:
AROMA:	AROMA:
TASTE:	TASTE:
POTENCY:	POTENCY:
EFFECT:	EFFECT:
APPEARANCE:	APPEARANCE:

STRAIN SUMMARY

STR:

THC: CBD:

INDICA/SATIVA:

AROMA:

TASTE:

POTENCY:

EFFECT:

APPEARANCE:

STR:

THC: CBD:

INDICA/SATIVA:

AROMA:

TASTE:

POTENCY:

EFFECT:

APPEARANCE:

STR:

THC: CBD:

INDICA/SATIVA:

AROMA:

TASTE:

POTENCY:

EFFECT:

APPEARANCE:

STR:

THC: CBD:

INDICA/SATIVA:

AROMA:

TASTE:

POTENCY:

EFFECT:

APPEARANCE:

STR:

THC: CBD:

INDICA/SATIVA:

AROMA:

TASTE:

POTENCY:

EFFECT:

APPEARANCE:

STR:

THC: CBD:

INDICA/SATIVA:

AROMA:

TASTE:

POTENCY:

EFFECT:

APPEARANCE:

Strain Summary

STR: THC: CBD: INDICA/SATIVA: AROMA: TASTE: POTENCY: EFFECT: APPEARANCE:	STR: THC: CBD: INDICA/SATIVA: AROMA: TASTE: POTENCY: EFFECT: APPEARANCE:
STR: THC: CBD: INDICA/SATIVA: AROMA: TASTE: POTENCY: EFFECT: APPEARANCE:	STR: THC: CBD: INDICA/SATIVA: AROMA: TASTE: POTENCY: EFFECT: APPEARANCE:
STR: THC: CBD: INDICA/SATIVA: AROMA: TASTE: POTENCY: EFFECT: APPEARANCE:	STR: THC: CBD: INDICA/SATIVA: AROMA: TASTE: POTENCY: EFFECT: APPEARANCE:

STRAIN SUMMARY

STR:	STR:
THC: CBD:	THC: CBD:
INDICA/SATIVA:	INDICA/SATIVA:
AROMA:	AROMA:
TASTE:	TASTE:
POTENCY:	POTENCY:
EFFECT:	EFFECT:
APPEARANCE:	APPEARANCE:
STR:	STR:
THC: CBD:	THC: CBD:
INDICA/SATIVA:	INDICA/SATIVA:
AROMA:	AROMA:
TASTE:	TASTE:
POTENCY:	POTENCY:
EFFECT:	EFFECT:
APPEARANCE:	APPEARANCE:
STR:	STR:
THC: CBD:	THC: CBD:
INDICA/SATIVA:	INDICA/SATIVA:
AROMA:	AROMA:
TASTE:	TASTE:
POTENCY:	POTENCY:
EFFECT:	EFFECT:
APPEARANCE:	APPEARANCE:

DISTRIBUTION

YOU CAN USE the following chart to keep track of finished product. It provides a space to log information such as where a product has gone, how much was received, and what's on consignment. The phrase "Funds Received" is used here to represent funds received for the services provided to produce a product that has been exchanged. "Pending" stands for the amount of funds you expect to receive for producing a product that's out on consignment. The term "Weight" is used for how many grams, ounces, or pounds were exchanged. When logging the strain of the product in question, use the number of the plant and the strain's initials or whichever label you prefer. The initials "MB" can be used when referring to a mix of buds of the same strain but from different plants, and "MS" can be used when referring to a mix of different strains. List who received the product or where it went under the term "Where." Use initials when filling in the "Where" space, and make a note on the bottom of the page to display what the initials stand for.

This template is primarily to serve as a guide and can be tailored to meet your specific needs. For example if you prefer to leave out the specific plant and strain or if the date is not important to you then you would just fill in the weight of what went out, what was received and if necessary where it went. The most important data would probably be the quantity of what went out and how much was received. This kind of information can help to eliminate confusion and to keep an awareness of what has been exchanged or not.

In the following example #7 BB stands for a Blueberry plant that was labeled #7; #9 KSH stands for a Kush plant labeled #9. MB = mixed buds, and MS = mixed strains.

Note: Once you've received funds for a consigned product, simply mark a check next to the amount pending.

Example:

FUNDS RECEIVED					ON CONSIGNMENT				
Strain	**Weight**	**Received**	**Date**	**Where**	**Strain**	**Weight**	**Pending**	**Date**	**Where**
#7 BB	2.5 lb	$1,800	11/09/18	MCC	#9KSH	1 lb	$800	11/3/18	MCC
MB/AFG	4 lb	$2,800	12/21/18	MCC	MS	2 lb	$1400	12/29/18	MCC

MCC = My cannabis club

FORM F-5

FUNDS RECEIVED

ON CONSIGNMENT

Strain	Weight	Received	Date	Where	Strain	Weight	Pending	Date	Where

FORM F-5

FUNDS RECEIVED					ON CONSIGNMENT				
Strain	Weight	Received	Date	Where	Strain	Weight	Pending	Date	Where

GENERAL NOTES

Products Purchased

Throughout the year, record all the products you've bought that pertain to the project. Include quantity, price, and date of purchase (save all store receipts). Share any details about the products' quality and effectiveness.

DAILY TO-DO LIST

YOU CAN USE the following pages as daily to-do lists or as scratch sheets for just about anything from shopping lists to what movie you want to see on the weekend.

DAILY TO-DO LIST

DAILY TO-DO LIST

DAILY TO-DO LIST

DAILY TO-DO LIST

DAILY TO-DO LIST

DAILY TO-DO LIST

DAILY TO-DO LIST

DAILY TO-DO LIST

DAILY TO-DO LIST

Daily To-Do List

GLOSSARY

cola buds: The terminal flower growing from the apex of each primary branch.

sexing: The process of identifying a plants gender.

stretch: When the stem of a flower cluster, otherwise known as the bud, begins to grow. This in turn causes the cluster to become loose.

strip: the act of removing a plants foliation

stripped: A plant that has been defoliated.

1sts: Firsts are the first buds to be harvested; usually consisting solely of the cola buds.

2nds: Seconds are the medium sized flowers cut during the 2nd harvest.

3rds: Thirds are the smaller flowers harvested after the 1sts and 2nds

About the Author

ALLAN J. GRAJEK began his agricultural journey in 1997 while exploring biodynamic farming practices. Known as a "plant whisperer," he has a keen eye and a natural intuition for gardening, combined with an aptitude for order and efficiency. Allan has devised effective methods for success in the cannabis industry, and has been consulting and training cannabis farmers since his arrival in Mendocino, California. He believes that orderly methods and detailed record keeping are vital to success, and many grateful clients have asked him to publish his approach to cultivation for the betterment of their industry. The father of two remarkable young men, Allan has lived in Mendocino for over thirteen years.